EMMANUEL JOSEPH

Decide with Heart, How Creativity and Self-Compassion Guide Better Choices and Stronger Connections

Copyright © 2025 by Emmanuel Joseph

All rights reserved. No part of this publication may be reproduced, stored or transmitted in any form or by any means, electronic, mechanical, photocopying, recording, scanning, or otherwise without written permission from the publisher. It is illegal to copy this book, post it to a website, or distribute it by any other means without permission.

First edition

This book was professionally typeset on Reedsy.
Find out more at reedsy.com

Contents

1	Chapter 1: The Essence of Creativity and Self-Compassion	1
2	Chapter 2: The Art of Mindful Decision-Making	3
3	Chapter 3: Embracing Imperfection	5
4	Chapter 4: The Power of Vulnerability	7
5	Chapter 5: The Role of Self-Reflection	9
6	Chapter 6: The Role of Empathy in Decision-Making	11
7	Chapter 7: The Intersection of Creativity and...	13
8	Chapter 8: The Power of Positive Affirmations	15
9	Chapter 9: Harnessing the Power of Visualization	17
10	Chapter 10: The Role of Gratitude in Decision-Making	19
11	Chapter 11: The Role of Intuition in Decision-Making	21
12	Chapter 12: The Role of Play in Creativity	23
13	Chapter 13: The Importance of Rest and Renewal	25
14	Chapter 14: The Role of Community and Connection	27
15	Chapter 15: The Power of Self-Awareness	29
16	Chapter 16: The Role of Purpose and Meaning	31
17	Chapter 17: The Journey of Self-Discovery	33

1

Chapter 1: The Essence of Creativity and Self-Compassion

Creativity and self-compassion are the twin engines that propel us toward more fulfilling lives. Creativity is not merely the domain of artists but an essential human trait that enables us to solve problems, express ourselves, and innovate. It is the mental agility that allows us to see possibilities where others see obstacles. Self-compassion, on the other hand, is the practice of treating ourselves with the same kindness and understanding we would extend to a friend. It is recognizing our shared humanity, acknowledging our imperfections, and embracing ourselves as we are. Together, these qualities form a powerful duo that guides our choices and enriches our connections with others.

When we approach decisions with a creative mindset, we open ourselves to a world of options. Creativity breaks the shackles of conventional thinking and empowers us to explore alternative solutions. It fosters a sense of curiosity and wonder, encouraging us to ask "what if?" and "why not?" This mindset transforms challenges into opportunities and failures into lessons. By embracing creativity, we become more adaptable and resilient, capable of navigating life's uncertainties with confidence and grace.

Self-compassion complements creativity by grounding us in a supportive inner dialogue. It helps us cultivate a sense of inner peace and stability, which is crucial when faced with difficult decisions. Instead of harsh self-criticism, self-compassion encourages us to treat ourselves with kindness and understanding. It reminds us that mistakes are part of the human experience and that we are worthy of love and acceptance, regardless of our shortcomings. This nurturing attitude creates a safe space for creative exploration, free from the fear of failure.

The synergy between creativity and self-compassion is profound. When we harness these qualities, we make decisions that are not only innovative but also aligned with our true selves. Our choices become a reflection of our values, passions, and aspirations. We are more likely to pursue paths that bring us joy and fulfillment, rather than conforming to external expectations. Moreover, the practice of self-compassion fosters stronger connections with others, as we become more empathetic and understanding. In essence, creativity and self-compassion guide us toward better choices and deeper, more meaningful relationships.

2

Chapter 2: The Art of Mindful Decision-Making

Mindful decision-making is an art that requires us to be fully present and engaged in the moment. It involves paying attention to our thoughts, feelings, and bodily sensations without judgment. By cultivating mindfulness, we create a space between stimulus and response, allowing us to make choices that are thoughtful and deliberate. This practice enhances our awareness of the various factors influencing our decisions, including our biases, emotions, and external pressures. As a result, we become more attuned to our true desires and values, making decisions that are authentic and intentional.

One of the key benefits of mindfulness is its ability to reduce stress and anxiety. When we are mindful, we are less likely to be overwhelmed by negative thoughts and emotions. Instead, we observe them with a sense of curiosity and detachment, allowing them to pass without being consumed by them. This calm and centered state of mind enables us to approach decisions with clarity and confidence. We are better equipped to weigh the pros and cons, consider multiple perspectives, and anticipate potential outcomes. In this way, mindfulness enhances our decision-making process and leads to more balanced and thoughtful choices.

Mindfulness also fosters a deeper connection with our inner wisdom. By quieting the mental chatter and distractions, we can tune into our intuition and gut feelings. These inner signals often provide valuable insights that logic and reasoning alone may not reveal. When we trust our intuition, we are more likely to make choices that resonate with our authentic selves. This alignment between our inner and outer worlds brings a sense of harmony and fulfillment to our lives. Moreover, mindfulness helps us stay open to new experiences and possibilities, fueling our creativity and expanding our horizons.

Practicing mindful decision-making requires ongoing effort and commitment. It is not a one-time event but a continuous journey of self-discovery and growth. We can cultivate mindfulness through various techniques, such as meditation, deep breathing, and mindful observation. By integrating these practices into our daily lives, we build a foundation of awareness and presence that supports us in making better choices. Over time, mindful decision-making becomes a natural and intuitive process, guiding us toward a life that is more intentional, creative, and compassionate.

3

Chapter 3: Embracing Imperfection

In a world that often glorifies perfection, embracing our imperfections can be a radical act of self-compassion. It involves recognizing that flaws and mistakes are part of the human experience and that they do not define our worth. When we accept ourselves as imperfect beings, we create space for growth and learning. We become more resilient in the face of challenges and more forgiving of our shortcomings. This attitude of self-acceptance fosters a sense of inner peace and contentment, allowing us to navigate life with greater ease and confidence.

One of the key benefits of embracing imperfection is the liberation it brings. When we let go of the need to be perfect, we free ourselves from the constraints of unrealistic expectations. We become more open to taking risks and exploring new possibilities. This willingness to step out of our comfort zones fuels our creativity and innovation. We are no longer held back by the fear of failure, but rather, we see failures as opportunities for growth and improvement. In this way, embracing imperfection empowers us to live more authentically and courageously.

Moreover, accepting our imperfections enhances our relationships with others. When we are compassionate toward ourselves, we become more empathetic and understanding toward others. We realize that everyone has their own struggles and that nobody is perfect. This realization fosters a sense of connection and solidarity, as we recognize our shared humanity. By embracing our imperfections, we create an environment of acceptance and support, where others feel safe to be their true selves. This strengthens our bonds and deepens our connections.

Practicing self-compassion and embracing imperfection is an ongoing journey. It requires us to be mindful of our self-talk and to challenge the inner critic that demands perfection. We can cultivate this practice through various techniques, such as positive affirmations, self-reflection, and seeking support from others. By nurturing a compassionate and accepting attitude toward ourselves, we build a strong foundation of self-love and resilience. This foundation supports us in making better decisions and forming stronger, more meaningful connections with others.

4

Chapter 4: The Power of Vulnerability

Vulnerability is often perceived as a weakness, but in reality, it is a source of great strength and courage. When we allow ourselves to be vulnerable, we open up to deeper connections and more authentic relationships. Vulnerability involves being honest about our feelings, fears, and insecurities. It means showing up as our true selves, without the masks and defenses that we often use to protect ourselves. By embracing vulnerability, we create space for genuine connection and intimacy with others.

One of the key aspects of vulnerability is the willingness to be seen and heard. When we share our true selves with others, we invite them to do the same. This mutual sharing creates a sense of trust and closeness, as we feel accepted and understood. Vulnerability breaks down the barriers that separate us and allows us to connect on a deeper level. It fosters a sense of belonging and community, as we recognize that we are not alone in our struggles and joys.

Vulnerability also plays a crucial role in creativity and innovation. When we are willing to take risks and share our ideas, we open ourselves to new possibilities. Creativity requires us to be open to failure and uncertainty, which can only happen when we embrace vulnerability. By being vulnerable, we give ourselves permission to experiment, explore, and make mistakes. This mindset fuels our creative potential and leads to innovative solutions and discoveries. In this way, vulnerability is a key driver of growth and progress.

Practicing vulnerability requires courage and mindfulness. It involves being present with our emotions and accepting them without judgment. We can cultivate vulnerability through various practices, such as journaling, sharing our feelings with trusted friends, and seeking support from others. By embracing vulnerability, we strengthen our emotional resilience and create more meaningful connections with others. This practice guides us toward a life that is more authentic, compassionate, and fulfilling.

5

Chapter 5: The Role of Self-Reflection

Self-reflection is a powerful tool for personal growth and decision-making. It involves taking the time to pause, look inward, and examine our thoughts, feelings, and experiences. Through self-reflection, we gain insights into our values, motivations, and patterns of behavior. This increased self-awareness allows us to make more informed and intentional choices that align with our true selves. By regularly engaging in self-reflection, we create a habit of continuous learning and growth.

One of the key benefits of self-reflection is its ability to clarify our goals and aspirations. When we take the time to reflect on what truly matters to us, we become more focused and purposeful in our actions. Self-reflection helps us identify our strengths and areas for improvement, guiding us toward personal and professional development. It also allows us to evaluate our progress and make adjustments as needed, ensuring that we stay on the path that is most fulfilling for us.

Self-reflection also enhances our emotional intelligence and resilience. By examining our emotional responses and triggers, we gain a deeper understanding of ourselves and our interactions with others. This awareness enables us to manage our emotions more effectively and respond to challenges with greater composure and empathy. Self-reflection helps us identify and address negative thought patterns and behaviors, fostering a more positive and constructive mindset. In this way, self-reflection supports our overall well-being and personal growth.

Practicing self-reflection requires dedication and mindfulness. We can cultivate this practice through various techniques, such as journaling, meditation, and seeking feedback from others. By setting aside time for regular self-reflection, we create a space for introspection and self-discovery. This practice allows us to connect with our inner wisdom and make decisions that are aligned with our true values and aspirations. Over time, self-reflection becomes an integral part of our decision-making process, guiding us toward a life that is more intentional, creative, and compassionate.

6

Chapter 6: The Role of Empathy in Decision-Making

Empathy is the ability to understand and share the feelings of others. It is a key component of emotional intelligence and plays a crucial role in our decision-making process. When we approach decisions with empathy, we consider the perspectives and experiences of those affected by our choices. This compassionate mindset helps us make more thoughtful and inclusive decisions that foster positive relationships and create a sense of community. Empathy allows us to connect with others on a deeper level and build trust and understanding.

One of the key benefits of empathy is its ability to enhance our problem-solving skills. When we put ourselves in others' shoes, we gain a more comprehensive understanding of the situation and the needs of those involved. This broader perspective enables us to identify more effective and equitable solutions. Empathy also encourages collaboration and open communication, as people feel heard and valued. By fostering a sense of connection and mutual respect, empathy helps us navigate conflicts and find common ground.

Empathy also plays a vital role in our personal growth and self-compassion. When we are empathetic toward others, we become more aware of our own emotions and experiences. This self-awareness allows us to recognize and address our own needs and vulnerabilities. By practicing empathy, we develop a deeper understanding of ourselves and our relationships with others. This introspective process fosters self-compassion and emotional resilience, as we learn to navigate life's challenges with greater empathy and understanding.

Practicing empathy requires mindfulness and active listening. We can cultivate empathy through various techniques, such as perspective-taking, emotional validation, and seeking to understand others' experiences. By making a conscious effort to empathize with others, we create a more compassionate and connected world. This practice guides us toward better decision-making and stronger relationships, as we navigate life with greater empathy and compassion.

7

Chapter 7: The Intersection of Creativity and Self-Compassion

The intersection of creativity and self-compassion is a powerful space where innovation and self-care converge. When we nurture our creative potential with self-compassion, we create an environment that supports growth, exploration, and resilience. This synergy allows us to approach challenges with curiosity and an open mind, while also being gentle and forgiving with ourselves. By embracing both creativity and self-compassion, we unlock our full potential and lead more fulfilling lives.

One of the key benefits of this intersection is the freedom to experiment and take risks. Creativity thrives in an environment where mistakes are seen as opportunities for learning and growth. When we practice self-compassion, we are more likely to take risks and explore new ideas without the fear of failure. This mindset fosters innovation and creativity, as we feel supported and encouraged in our endeavors. By combining creativity and self-compassion, we create a space where we can dream big and pursue our passions with confidence.

Moreover, the intersection of creativity and self-compassion enhances our problem-solving skills. When we approach challenges with a creative mindset, we are more likely to find innovative solutions. Self-compassion supports this process by providing the emotional resilience needed to navigate setbacks and obstacles. By being kind and understanding with ourselves, we create a safe space for creative exploration and experimentation. This synergy allows us to tackle problems with creativity and compassion, leading to more effective and sustainable solutions.

Practicing the intersection of creativity and self-compassion requires mindfulness and intentionality. We can cultivate this practice through various techniques, such as creative journaling, meditation, and self-reflection. By integrating these practices into our daily lives, we build a foundation of creativity and self-compassion that supports our overall well-being and personal growth. This practice guides us toward better decision-making and stronger connections, as we navigate life with greater creativity and compassion.

8

Chapter 8: The Power of Positive Affirmations

Positive affirmations are powerful tools for cultivating a compassionate and empowering mindset. They are statements that reflect our values, goals, and aspirations, and they help us reframe negative thoughts and beliefs. By regularly practicing positive affirmations, we reinforce a positive self-image and build self-confidence. This mindset supports our decision-making process, as we approach challenges with greater optimism and resilience. Positive affirmations also enhance our overall well-being and personal growth.

One of the key benefits of positive affirmations is their ability to shift our focus from negative to positive thinking. When we repeat affirmations that reflect our strengths and potential, we create new neural pathways in the brain that reinforce these beliefs. This process helps us break free from limiting thought patterns and develop a more constructive and empowering mindset. Positive affirmations encourage us to see opportunities instead of obstacles, and to approach challenges with a sense of possibility and hope.

Positive affirmations also play a crucial role in self-compassion and emotional resilience. By affirming our worth and value, we develop a more compassionate and supportive inner dialogue. This self-affirming mindset helps us navigate setbacks and failures with greater grace and understanding.

Positive affirmations remind us that we are capable and deserving of success, regardless of our imperfections. This nurturing attitude fosters self-love and resilience, as we build a strong foundation of self-compassion and inner strength.

Practicing positive affirmations requires consistency and intentionality. We can integrate affirmations into our daily routine through various techniques, such as writing them down, repeating them aloud, or incorporating them into meditation and visualization practices. By making a conscious effort to practice positive affirmations, we create a more empowering and compassionate mindset. This practice guides us toward better decision-making and stronger connections, as we navigate life with greater self-confidence and optimism.

9

Chapter 9: Harnessing the Power of Visualization

Visualization is a powerful tool that allows us to create mental images of our goals and aspirations. By vividly imagining our desired outcomes, we activate the creative potential of our minds and align our actions with our intentions. Visualization helps us clarify our goals, boost our motivation, and enhance our performance. This practice supports our decision-making process by providing a clear and compelling vision of what we want to achieve.

One of the key benefits of visualization is its ability to enhance our focus and concentration. When we visualize our goals, we create a mental roadmap that guides our actions and decisions. This mental rehearsal helps us stay focused on our objectives and avoid distractions. Visualization also activates the same neural pathways in the brain that are involved in actual performance, enhancing our skills and abilities. By regularly practicing visualization, we improve our performance and increase our chances of success.

Visualization also plays a crucial role in building self-confidence and resilience. When we imagine ourselves achieving our goals, we reinforce a positive self-image and boost our confidence. Visualization helps us overcome self-doubt and fear by creating a sense of familiarity and comfort with our desired outcomes. This mental rehearsal prepares us to face challenges with greater resilience and determination. By visualizing success, we cultivate a positive mindset that supports our overall well-being and personal growth.

Practicing visualization requires mindfulness and intentionality. We can integrate visualization into our daily routine through various techniques, such as guided imagery, meditation, and vision boards. By making a conscious effort to visualize our goals, we create a clear and compelling vision of our future. This practice guides us toward better decision-making and stronger connections, as we navigate life with greater clarity and purpose.

10

Chapter 10: The Role of Gratitude in Decision-Making

Gratitude is the practice of recognizing and appreciating the positive aspects of our lives. It is a powerful mindset that enhances our overall well-being and supports our decision-making process. When we approach decisions with gratitude, we focus on the abundance and opportunities around us, rather than on what is lacking. This positive perspective helps us make more thoughtful and balanced choices that align with our values and aspirations.

One of the key benefits of gratitude is its ability to shift our focus from negativity to positivity. When we cultivate gratitude, we become more aware of the blessings and opportunities in our lives. This positive mindset helps us approach challenges with a sense of optimism and hope. Gratitude also enhances our resilience by providing a sense of perspective and grounding us in the present moment. By focusing on what we have, rather than on what we lack, we develop a more balanced and constructive approach to decision-making.

Gratitude also plays a crucial role in strengthening our relationships with others. When we express gratitude, we acknowledge and appreciate the contributions and support of those around us. This practice fosters a sense of connection and reciprocity, as people feel valued and appreciated. Gratitude enhances our empathy and understanding, as we recognize the positive impact others have on our lives. By cultivating gratitude, we create a more compassionate and supportive environment that strengthens our connections with others.

Practicing gratitude requires mindfulness and intentionality. We can integrate gratitude into our daily routine through various techniques, such as keeping a gratitude journal, expressing appreciation to others, and reflecting on positive experiences. By making a conscious effort to practice gratitude, we create a positive and empowering mindset. This practice guides us toward better decision-making and stronger connections, as we navigate life with greater appreciation and contentment.

11

Chapter 11: The Role of Intuition in Decision-Making

Intuition is the ability to understand or know something without conscious reasoning. It is a powerful and often underestimated tool in our decision-making process. When we trust our intuition, we tap into our inner wisdom and gain insights that logic and reasoning alone may not reveal. Intuition helps us make quick and confident decisions, especially in situations where we have limited information or time. By cultivating our intuition, we enhance our overall decision-making skills and navigate life with greater confidence and ease.

One of the key benefits of intuition is its ability to provide valuable insights and guidance. Intuition draws on our past experiences, knowledge, and subconscious mind to offer solutions and perspectives that may not be immediately apparent. This inner knowing helps us navigate complex and uncertain situations with greater clarity and confidence. Intuition also enhances our creativity and problem-solving skills, as it encourages us to think outside the box and explore new possibilities.

Intuition also plays a crucial role in self-compassion and emotional resilience. When we trust our intuition, we develop a deeper connection with ourselves and our inner wisdom. This self-awareness helps us recognize and honor our true desires and needs. By trusting our intuition, we create a sense of alignment and harmony between our inner and outer worlds. This practice fosters self-compassion and emotional resilience, as we navigate life's challenges with greater trust and confidence.

Practicing intuition requires mindfulness and intentionality. We can cultivate our intuition through various techniques, such as meditation, journaling, and paying attention to our gut feelings. By making a conscious effort to listen to our intuition, we create a deeper connection with our inner wisdom. This practice guides us toward better decision-making and stronger connections, as we navigate life with greater intuition and insight.

12

Chapter 12: The Role of Play in Creativity

Play is a fundamental aspect of human experience and a powerful catalyst for creativity. When we engage in play, we activate our imagination and explore new possibilities. Play allows us to experiment, take risks, and learn through discovery. It fosters a sense of curiosity and wonder, which are essential for creative thinking. By incorporating play into our lives, we nurture our creative potential and enhance our overall well-being.

One of the key benefits of play is its ability to reduce stress and promote relaxation. Play allows us to take a break from our daily responsibilities and immerse ourselves in enjoyable activities. This mental and emotional respite helps us recharge and rejuvenate, making us more productive and focused. Play also enhances our problem-solving skills by encouraging us to think outside the box and approach challenges with a fresh perspective. By fostering a playful mindset, we become more open to new ideas and more adaptable in the face of change.

Play also strengthens our connections with others. When we engage in playful activities with friends and family, we create shared experiences and memories. Play fosters a sense of joy and camaraderie, as we laugh and bond with others. This sense of connection and belonging enhances our overall well-being and emotional resilience. Play also encourages collaboration and teamwork, as we work together to achieve common goals. By incorporating play into our lives, we create a more balanced and fulfilling life.

Practicing play requires intentionality and mindfulness. We can incorporate play into our daily routine through various activities, such as games, sports, creative projects, and hobbies. By making a conscious effort to engage in play, we nurture our creativity and enhance our overall well-being. This practice guides us toward better decision-making and stronger connections, as we navigate life with greater joy and creativity.

13

Chapter 13: The Importance of Rest and Renewal

Rest and renewal are essential for our overall well-being and creative potential. When we take the time to rest and recharge, we enhance our physical, mental, and emotional health. Rest allows us to recover from the demands of daily life and restore our energy and vitality. It also fosters creativity and innovation, as our minds have the opportunity to wander and explore new ideas. By prioritizing rest and renewal, we create a foundation of well-being that supports our personal and professional growth.

One of the key benefits of rest is its ability to enhance our cognitive functioning and productivity. When we are well-rested, we are more focused, alert, and efficient. Rest also improves our problem-solving skills and creativity, as our minds have the opportunity to process and integrate new information. By taking regular breaks and getting enough sleep, we enhance our overall performance and decision-making abilities. Rest is not a luxury but a necessity for our overall well-being and success.

Rest also plays a crucial role in our emotional resilience and self-compassion. When we are well-rested, we are better equipped to manage stress and navigate challenges with greater ease. Rest allows us to recharge our emotional reserves and cultivate a sense of inner peace and stability. By prioritizing rest and renewal, we create a supportive environment for self-compassion and emotional well-being. This practice fosters a sense of balance and harmony in our lives, as we navigate life's demands with greater resilience and grace.

Practicing rest and renewal requires intentionality and mindfulness. We can cultivate this practice through various techniques, such as meditation, deep breathing, and regular sleep. By making a conscious effort to prioritize rest, we enhance our overall well-being and creative potential. This practice guides us toward better decision-making and stronger connections, as we navigate life with greater energy and vitality.

14

Chapter 14: The Role of Community and Connection

Community and connection are fundamental aspects of human experience and essential for our overall well-being. When we cultivate strong connections with others, we create a sense of belonging and support. Community provides us with a network of relationships that enrich our lives and enhance our resilience. By fostering a sense of connection and community, we create a supportive environment that nurtures our personal and professional growth.

One of the key benefits of community is its ability to provide emotional support and encouragement. When we are connected with others, we have a sense of security and comfort. Community provides us with a safe space to share our experiences, challenges, and triumphs. This support helps us navigate life's ups and downs with greater resilience and confidence. By cultivating strong connections with others, we enhance our emotional well-being and overall happiness.

Community also plays a crucial role in our creativity and innovation. When we are connected with others, we have access to diverse perspectives and ideas. Community fosters collaboration and teamwork, as we work together to achieve common goals. This collaborative environment enhances our creativity and problem-solving skills, as we learn from and inspire each other.

By fostering a sense of community, we create a more dynamic and innovative environment that supports our personal and professional growth.

Practicing community and connection requires intentionality and mindfulness. We can cultivate this practice through various activities, such as joining clubs, volunteering, and participating in social events. By making a conscious effort to connect with others, we create a supportive and enriching environment. This practice guides us toward better decision-making and stronger connections, as we navigate life with greater support and camaraderie.

15

Chapter 15: The Power of Self-Awareness

Self-awareness is the ability to recognize and understand our thoughts, feelings, and behaviors. It is a fundamental aspect of emotional intelligence and plays a crucial role in our decision-making process. When we cultivate self-awareness, we gain insights into our values, motivations, and patterns of behavior. This increased self-awareness allows us to make more informed and intentional choices that align with our true selves.

One of the key benefits of self-awareness is its ability to enhance our emotional intelligence and resilience. When we are aware of our emotions and triggers, we can manage our responses more effectively. This self-awareness helps us navigate challenges with greater composure and empathy. Self-awareness also enhances our relationships with others, as we become more attuned to their feelings and experiences. By cultivating self-awareness, we create a more balanced and harmonious life.

Self-awareness also plays a crucial role in our personal growth and self-compassion. When we are aware of our strengths and areas for improvement, we can make intentional efforts to develop and grow. This self-awareness fosters a sense of self-compassion, as we recognize and honor our true selves. By practicing self-awareness, we create a supportive environment for personal and professional growth. This practice enhances our overall well-being and guides us toward better decision-making and stronger connections.

Practicing self-awareness requires mindfulness and intentionality. We can cultivate this practice through various techniques, such as journaling, meditation, and seeking feedback from others. By making a conscious effort to practice self-awareness, we create a deeper connection with ourselves and our inner wisdom. This practice guides us toward better decision-making and stronger connections, as we navigate life with greater self-awareness and insight.

16

Chapter 16: The Role of Purpose and Meaning

Purpose and meaning are essential aspects of a fulfilling life. When we have a clear sense of purpose, we are more motivated, focused, and resilient. Purpose provides us with a sense of direction and guides our decisions and actions. It helps us navigate challenges and setbacks with greater determination and perseverance. By cultivating a sense of purpose, we create a life that is meaningful and aligned with our values and aspirations.

One of the key benefits of purpose is its ability to enhance our overall well-being and satisfaction. When we engage in activities that align with our purpose, we experience a sense of fulfillment and joy. Purpose gives our lives meaning and significance, as we contribute to something greater than ourselves. This sense of meaning fosters emotional resilience and self-compassion, as we recognize the value and impact of our actions. By living with purpose, we create a more meaningful and satisfying life.

Purpose also plays a crucial role in our decision-making process. When we have a clear sense of purpose, we are better equipped to make choices that align with our values and goals. Purpose provides us with a framework for evaluating our options and determining the best course of action. It helps us stay focused on our long-term objectives and avoid distractions. By cultivating a sense of purpose, we make more intentional and informed decisions that support our overall well-being and personal growth.

Practicing purpose and meaning requires mindfulness and intentionality. We can cultivate this practice through various techniques, such as setting goals, reflecting on our values, and seeking opportunities for growth and contribution. By making a conscious effort to live with purpose, we create a life that is meaningful and fulfilling. This practice guides us toward better decision-making and stronger connections, as we navigate life with greater purpose and clarity.

17

Chapter 17: The Journey of Self-Discovery

Self-discovery is a lifelong journey of exploring and understanding our true selves. It involves recognizing our strengths, values, passions, and aspirations. Self-discovery allows us to connect with our authentic selves and live a life that is true to who we are. By embarking on this journey, we gain insights into our motivations and patterns of behavior, guiding us toward personal and professional growth.

One of the key benefits of self-discovery is its ability to enhance our self-awareness and emotional intelligence. When we take the time to explore our inner world, we gain a deeper understanding of our thoughts, feelings, and behaviors. This self-awareness helps us navigate challenges with greater resilience and empathy. Self-discovery also fosters self-compassion, as we recognize and honor our true selves. By embracing our uniqueness, we create a more balanced and harmonious life.

Self-discovery also plays a crucial role in our decision-making process. When we are connected with our authentic selves, we make choices that align with our values and aspirations. Self-discovery provides us with a clear sense of direction and purpose, guiding our decisions and actions. It helps us stay true to ourselves and avoid conforming to external expectations. By embarking on the journey of self-discovery, we make more intentional and informed decisions that support our overall well-being and personal growth.

Practicing self-discovery requires mindfulness and intentionality. We can cultivate this practice through various techniques, such as journaling, meditation, and seeking feedback from others. By making a conscious effort to explore and understand ourselves, we create a deeper connection with our inner wisdom. This practice guides us toward better decision-making and stronger connections, as we navigate life with greater self-awareness and authenticity.

Book Description:

Decide with Heart: How Creativity and Self-Compassion Guide Better Choices and Stronger Connections is a transformative guide that explores the powerful synergy between creativity and self-compassion. Drawing from psychological insights, practical exercises, and real-life stories, this book empowers readers to harness their creative potential and cultivate a compassionate mindset. Through mindful decision-making, embracing imperfection, and fostering meaningful connections, readers will discover how to navigate life's challenges with greater clarity, confidence, and resilience. **Decide with Heart** is an invitation to live more authentically, make choices that resonate with our true selves, and build stronger, more fulfilling relationships.

www.ingramcontent.com/pod-product-compliance
Lightning Source LLC
LaVergne TN
LVHW020457080526
838202LV00057B/6010